Alexander Graham BELL

Stewart Ross

RAINTREE
STECK-VAUGHN
PUBLISHERS

A Harcourt Company

Austin   New York
www.raintreesteckvaughn.com

BESSEMER PUBLIC LIBRARY

© Copyright 2001, text, Steck-Vaughn Company

All rights reserved. No part of this book may be reproduced or utilized in any form or by any means, electronic or mechanical, including photocopying, recording or by any information storage and retrieval system, without permission in writing from the Publishers. Inquiries should be addressed to: Copyright Permissions, Steck-Vaughn Company, P.O. Box 26015, Austin, TX 78755.

Published by Raintree Steck-Vaughn Publishers,
an imprint of Steck-Vaughn Company

Library of Congress Cataloging-in-Publication Data

Ross Stewart.
    Alexander Graham Bell / Stewart Ross.
        p. cm. -- (Scientists who made history)
    ISBN 0-7398-4415-6
        1. Bell, Alexander Graham, 1847-1922--Juvenile literature. 2.Inventors--United States--Biography --Juvenile literature. [1. Bell, Alexander Graham, 1847-1922. 2. Inventors.] I. Title II. Series.

    TK6143.B4 R67 2001
    621.385'092--dc21
    [B]   2001019210

Printed in Italy. Bound in the United States.

1 2 3 4 5 6 7 8 9 0 LB 05 04 03 02 01

Picture Acknowledgements: Corbis 4, 9, 11, 21, 35, 38, 40 (top), 42, 43 (top & bottom); ET Archive 39; Mary Evans 8, 14, 16, 19, 22, 28, 30, 30-31, 34; Hodder Wayland Picture Library 9 (top), 25 (top & bottom), 29, 32 (top & bottom), 43 (bottom); Peter Newark 6, 7; Parks Canada, Alexander Graham Bell National Historic Site 12, 15 (bottom), 17, 36, 37; Photri 26, 41; Science Museum 5, 10, 18, 24, 33; Smithsonian Institute 23; Still Moving Picture Company 15 (top).

Contents

Speech Down a Wire

IT IS THE afternoon of Friday March 10, 1876. In a small apartment in Exeter Place, Boston, Massachusetts, a tall young man with sideburns and long black hair is leaning over a wooden table. Before him stands a dish of weak acid. Around it are scattered lengths of wire, bottles, batteries, clips, papers, and other pieces of scientific apparatus.

BELOW: *A reconstruction of Alexander Graham Bell's laboratory as it looked in 1876. The Bell model is holding a receiver connected by wires to a copper tube standing in a jar of acid.*

A curved metal tube is suspended over the dish. From its covered end, a thin needle dips into the acid. A wire attached to the needle leads across the table, under the closed laboratory door, and down the hall to the bedroom. Here the wire is attached to a crude receiver. Thomas Watson, a small bearded man with a high forehead, sits with the receiver pushed hard against his ear.

The bedroom door is shut. Two wires are attached to the receiver. The second runs back, via a battery, to a copper tube standing in the dish of acid. The experiment is ready.

The young scientist in the laboratory stands up from the table and listens. Not a sound. He takes a deep breath, bends forward and calls loudly into the open end of the metal tube: "Mr. Watson, come here. I want to see you." His clear voice has a marked Scottish accent. When he has finished speaking, he stands back and waits to see what will happen.

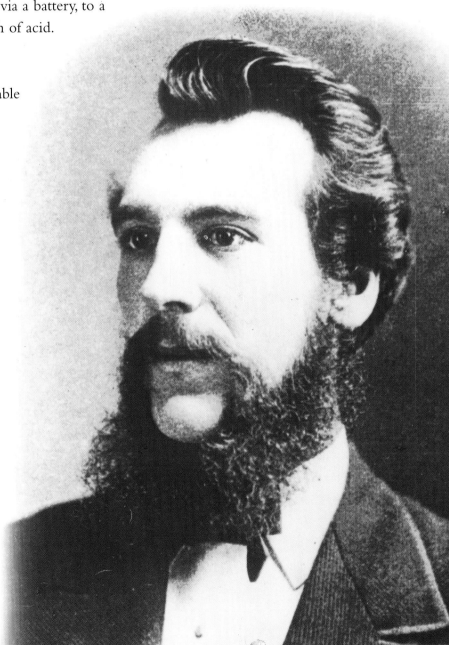

RIGHT: *Alexander Graham Bell as a young man. This photograph was taken in the same year that he invented the telephone, in 1876.*

The bedroom door opens with a click. Quick footsteps echo along the hallway. The laboratory door is flung open and Watson comes in, grinning broadly.

"Yes, Mr. Watson?" asks the young scientist, his dark eyes bright with excitement.

"I heard you, Mr. Bell," Watson replies eagerly. "I heard you and I came straight away."

Alexander Graham Bell raises his hand.

"Wait! We must be sure there was no mistake. What did you hear, Watson? What were my exact words?"

"You said: 'Mr. Watson, come here. I want to see you.' I heard it clearly through the receiver."

Bell claps his hands in delight. "Wonderful! Speech down a wire!" He walks quickly to the laboratory door. "Now it's your turn, Watson. Wait until I'm in the bedroom, then read something into the voice tube." He hurries out of the room, shutting the door behind him.

LEFT: *This print of Broadway, New York City in 1880 shows the criss-cross of telephone and telegraph wires that had appeared only four years after Bell's invention of the telephone.*

BESSEMER PUBLIC LIBRARY

IN THEIR OWN WORDS

"I feel that at last I have struck the solution of a great problem—and the day is coming when telegraph wires will be laid on to houses just like water or gas —and friends converse with each other without leaving home."

ALEXANDER GRAHAM BELL IN A LETTER TO HIS FATHER, DATED MARCH 10, 1876, REALIZING HOW HIS INVENTION WOULD AFFECT EVERYONE'S LIVES.

BELOW: *Happy New Year! Guests at a New Year's Eve party in 1880 exchange greetings with distant friends by telephone.*

After a short pause, Watson takes up a book and reads a few passages into the voice tube. When he has finished, he says slowly, "Mr. Bell, do you understand what I say? Do - you - un - der - stand - what - I - say?"

As soon as Watson has finished, Bell rushes back to the laboratory. "Yes, it works!" he cries, grabbing his assistant by the hand. "We've done it! I didn't get every word. But I could hear most of them and all of the last sentence. Speech by telegraph, Watson! This will change the world!"

Alexander Graham Bell was right. Although only 29 years old, he had made one of the greatest inventions of modern times. "Speech by telegraph" is what we now call the telephone.

BESSEMER PUBLIC LIBRARY

Science and Scotland

ON MARCH 3, 1847, a second son was born to Alexander Melville Bell and his wife Eliza Grace. The baby was christened Alexander, like his father, although in the family he was known as Aleck. Eleven years later, in honor of a family friend, he was given the additional name of Graham.

Aleck was born in Edinburgh, the capital of Scotland. Here he received his early education, first from his parents, and then at respected local schools. Scotland was famous for the emphasis it placed on education, which put it far in advance of its richer neighbor, England. Aleck Bell, bright and eager to learn, was one of many Scots who benefited from the care the Scots lavished on their children. He was also fortunate to spend his early years in Edinburgh. The city, commonly known as the "Athens of the North," was a major European center of science and learning. Its university was a world leader in medicine and several other subjects.

BELOW: *A view over the city of Edinburgh, Scotland, in 1879. Charlotte Street, where Bell was born, is to the right of the main street, shown here.*

Scotland had a fine reputation for engineering. It had produced many of the more important technological advances of the 18th and early 19th centuries. Thomas Telford had transformed the art of road building. Kirkpatrick MacMillan built the world's first bicycle. Most significant of all, James Watt developed the steam engine, the workhorse of the Industrial Revolution. Better roads, bicycles, and steam locomotives all helped change the speed of transportation and communications. At the same time, an even more dramatic method of communication was appearing—the telegraph.

ABOVE: *Thomas Telford (1757–1834), the great Scottish engineer who oversaw the construction of more than 2,560 miles (1,600 km) of road and 1,200 bridges. One of his bridges has been painted in the background of the portrait.*

BELOW: *Passengers crowded into lower-class accommodation, at the back of a steam train on the Liverpool-to-Manchester line, in the late 19th century.*

COMMUNICATION

For thousands of years, human beings had communicated over short distances through sound (using speech or musical instruments) and sight (using hand movements or flags). Long-distance communication meant moving an object (either as a messenger or a letter) from one place to another. The speed of communication depended on how quickly this person or object could be moved.

The Telegraph

Ten years before Aleck Bell's birth, the American professor Samuel Morse demonstrated to the U.S. government how messages could be sent using electricity and a device called a telegraph. This device, which had been developed by a number of different scientists, involved passing electrical signals down a wire. Morse had devised a code of signals, called the Morse Code, which represented letters of the alphabet. This enabled messages in words to be sent swiftly over long distances.

RIGHT: *Samuel Morse (1791–1872) was an American inventor who created the telegraph and the famous Morse Code.*

The first successful electric telegraph was made in 1837 by the British inventors Sir Charles Wheatstone and Sir William Cooke. Later that year, Samuel Morse developed his telegraph in the United States. The telegraph used an electric current transmitted down a wire to send messages from place to place.

(1) The telegraph operator pressed a key to start the electric circuit and released the key to break the circuit. This sent pulses of electricity down the wire.

(2) Depending on how long the operator pressed the key, the pulses of electricity varied in duration.

(3) The pulses of current delivered a message either as a code (such as the Morse Code) or by moving a pointer to give a visual signal. On May 24, 1844, the first message sent was "What hath God wrought?"

MORSE'S TELEGRAPH TRANSMITTER

Moving arm started and broke electric circuit.

The telegraph had two drawbacks. First, it relied on trained operators to send and receive coded messages. Second, telegraph messages were entirely in writing. What was needed was a way of sending speech down the wire rather than electrical signals. However, although it seemed an obvious development, it baffled scientists for years.

ABOVE: *This telegraph transmitter was used to send the first telegraph message from Washington, D.C., to Baltimore, on May 24, 1844.*

SPEECH

The Bell family had long been interested in sound and speech. Aleck's grandfather (another Alexander) was a shoemaker who turned to acting. Having learned to speak clearly through acting, he began giving elocution lessons. He gained such a good reputation for teaching that he was able to move to London and carry on teaching. He also wrote books about speaking correctly and how to cure a stammer.

Aleck's father, Alexander Melville, followed in his father's footsteps, but his approach was more scientific. He studied the physics of sound, focusing on how the voice sounds when saying vowels and consonants. Later, his book *The Standard Elocutionist* became an international best-seller. It earned a fortune for the publisher, but not for the author.

Deafness

Aleck's father also studied deafness and became fascinated by ways to help deaf people to speak. He invented a system called "Visible Speech," which was a code of symbols indicating the position of the throat, tongue, and lips when making sounds. By following the symbols, a deaf person could arrange their mouth and tongue to produce a particular sound.

BELOW: *Alexander Bell (1790–1865), Alexander Graham Bell's grandfather. A specialist in speech therapy, he had a strong influence on his grandson's development.*

Visible Speech was never as widely used as Alexander Melville had hoped. However, it certainly helped many of his deaf pupils, and his work on the physics of sound had a profound influence on his son. Aleck grew up in a home where the making and transmission of sound was discussed almost daily.

The "New World"

Aleck learned other lessons in the family home. In 1838, his father had been sent to Newfoundland, Canada, to recover from illness. He returned in good health, convinced that in North America, the "New World," it was easier to recover from setbacks than in Britain. It was an opinion that Aleck came to share.

IN THEIR OWN WORDS

"You will have cause of thankfulness all your life that you had the benefit of such a training as my father has lovingly afforded you."

ALECK'S FATHER, ALEXANDER MELVILLE BELL, WRITING TO HIS SON WHEN ALECK WAS IN LONDON, IN MARCH 1863.

VISIBLE SPEECH

Alexander Melville Bell's "Visible Speech" used a code of symbols to show deaf people how to position their throat, tongue, and lips to make sounds. This diagram shows the positions for three sounds, and the symbols for 1 to 8 below.

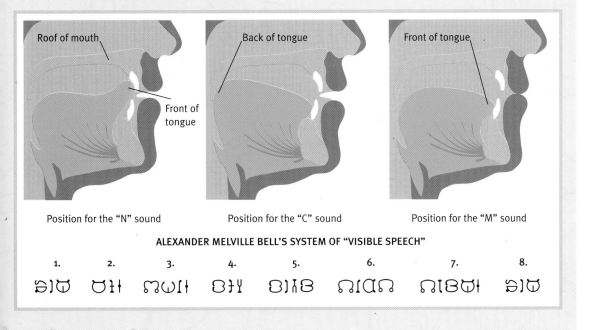

Position for the "N" sound

Position for the "C" sound

Position for the "M" sound

Roof of mouth

Front of tongue

Back of tongue

Front of tongue

ALEXANDER MELVILLE BELL'S SYSTEM OF "VISIBLE SPEECH"

1.   2.   3.   4.   5.   6.   7.   8.

The Teacher-Scientist

THE THREE BOYS in the Bell family were Aleck, his older brother Melville ("Melly"), and his younger brother Edward ("Ted"). They lived mostly in a rented apartment in South Charlotte Street, a street off Edinburgh's fashionable Charlotte Square. Here they had to dress neatly and keep quiet, as all well-brought-up children were expected to do in the 19th century.

Aleck's parents did not believe the city was a good environment for children. So, when he had saved a little money, Mr. Bell bought Milton Cottage in the country parish of Trinity. Whenever possible, the family escaped there to relax. They walked through the hills by day and played music and family games in the evenings. Aleck was a good piano player and actor. His favorite party piece was a "bee chase"—rushing frantically around the room after an imaginary bee until he caught it in his cupped hands.

BELOW: *The High Street, Edinburgh, in about 1840. Alexander Graham Bell's parents liked to get away from the crowded city into the countryside whenever they could.*

Before he went to school at the age of ten, Aleck's education was haphazard. Guided by his parents, he was encouraged to read widely, explore the city, ask endless questions, and even spend dreamy hours lying in the long grass. As a result, he grew up sharp and inquisitive, with a broad general knowledge, especially of scientific and technological matters. As history was to prove, it was an ideal upbringing for an inventor.

Aleck had only about four years of formal education. After a year at Hamilton Place Academy, he and Ted joined Melly at Edinburgh's Royal High School. Aleck proved a competent student, but that was it. He enjoyed Math, hated Latin and Greek, and won no prizes. In 1862, at the age of 15, he left school and traveled south to London to visit his grandfather.

ABOVE: *Aleck spent his childhood in an apartment in this building, in South Charlotte Street, Edinburgh.*

LEFT: *The Bell family in about 1857, when Aleck was 10 years old. His mother and father, Eliza and Alexander Melville Bell, sit in the center. Behind them, from left to right, are Aleck, Melville, and Edward.*

IN THEIR OWN WORDS

"We miss you sadly when we assemble by the fireside at the cottage, but we are reconciled to your absence by the fact that you are good to grandpa and have been a great comfort to him in his illness, and also that you are making good progress in your studies."

ALECK'S FATHER, ALEXANDER MELVILLE BELL, WRITING TO HIS SON WHILE ALECK WAS IN LONDON, IN MARCH 1863.

STARTING WORK

Aleck later described his year in London as "the turning point of my whole career." His grandfather, a wealthy and successful teacher of elocution, organized a program of private education for him, including reading widely, going to the theater, and learning to make speeches. He dressed him in fashionable clothes, too, and gave him a generous allowance. Guided by his grandfather, Aleck grew up fast, gaining confidence and learning the importance of intellectual discipline. He went to London a schoolboy, and returned home in 1863 a young man.

Before catching the train north, Aleck visited the British scientist Sir Charles Wheatstone. Like Aleck's father, Sir Charles was also interested in the mechanism of speech and had a talking machine, which he demonstrated to visitors. He had also invented a telegraph, so it was appropriate that the two should have met.

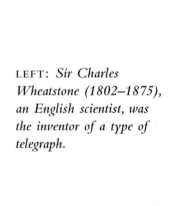

LEFT: *Sir Charles Wheatstone (1802–1875), an English scientist, was the inventor of a type of telegraph.*

Sixteen-year-old Aleck was bored in Edinburgh. He wanted independence and he wanted money. After working with his brother Melly on a speaking machine that made a realistic "Mama!" sound, he took a job teaching music and elocution at Weston House, a private boarding school for boys in Elgin, northeast Scotland. Meanwhile, Melly attended classes at Edinburgh University. In 1864, the brothers traded places. Melly taught in Elgin and Aleck went to the university. However, he learned very little and left after a few weeks.

Now a confident-looking young man with long, swept-back dark hair, Aleck returned to Elgin the following year at the age of 17. In his spare time, he began his first scientific experiments. Using tuning forks, he tried to find out the exact pitch of each vowel sound. His work was inspired by his father's Visible Speech alphabet, which had just appeared publicly.

RIGHT: *The confident and fashionable young Alexander Graham Bell, at the age of 16 or 17.*

THE TUNING FORK

The tuning fork is said to have been invented in 1711, by the English trumpeter John Shore. When a tuning fork is struck, it vibrates. This creates the sound waves, or vibrations in the air, that we hear. The pitch of the sound from a tuning fork depends on the length of its prongs. A long prong vibrates slowly, creating longer sound waves and a deeper sound.

TEACHING AND TUBERCULOSIS

In 1866, Aleck's father and mother moved to London and began promoting the Visible Speech program. Aleck, now aged 19, taught at Somersetshire College in Bath, in southwest England. Here, using homemade batteries, he rigged up one of Wheatstone's telegraphs between his house and that of a friend a few doors away. First sound, now electricity—gradually, Aleck was mastering the two basic elements of the telephone.

The following year, Aleck's younger brother, the 18-year-old Edward, died from tuberculosis. Aleck left Bath and joined his parents in London. Using his father's Visible Speech program, he taught at a school for deaf children. He also enrolled as a student at London University. In his spare time he experimented with the vibrations made by piano wires and dreamed of making an "electric piano."

BELOW: *Diagrams of the telegraph invented by Charles Wheatstone and William Cooke in 1837. Unlike Morse's telegraph, signals were received as visible movements of a needle.*

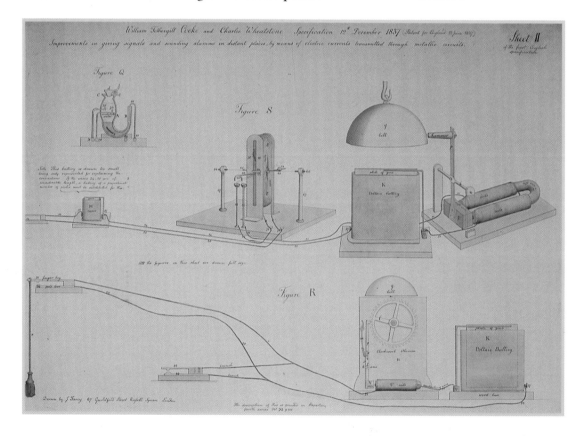

BESSEMER PUBLIC LIBRARY

LEFT: *Tuberculosis is the disease that killed both of Alexander Graham Bell's brothers. The German scientist Robert Koch attempts (unsuccessfully) to treat a patient with tuberculosis by using goat's blood in 1890.*

Meanwhile, Alexander Melville found the Americans more interested in Visible Speech than the British. In 1868, he had gone on a lecture tour of the United States. On his return, he suggested the whole family might emigrate. He believed there was more opportunity for original, hard-working people like the Bells in America than in Europe. Besides, it would do Aleck and Melly good to get out of foggy, damp London.

Although Aleck was unwell, Melly was worse, and on May 28, 1870, he died of tuberculosis in his parents' home. All doubts now vanished from Mr. Bell's mind. Two months later, accompanied by Eliza and Aleck, he boarded a steamer bound for the land where all setbacks could be overcome.

IN THEIR OWN WORDS

"Don't grieve about your examinations, etc.—all the degrees in the world would not make up for ill health....Make a name for yourself away. Don't get absorbed in yourself—mix freely with your fellows.... How I shall miss you all!... I scarcely expect you will return, England would be too slow for you after America."

FROM A LETTER TO ALECK FROM A FRIEND, MARIE ECCLESTON, ON JULY 2, 1870, JUST BEFORE HE LEFT FOR CANADA.

BESSEMER PUBLIC LIBRARY

Canada and the United States

ON AUGUST 1, 1870, the Bells arrived at Quebec, Canada and traveled to Brantford, Ontario. Here they settled into Tutelo Heights, a large house standing amid ten and a half acres of beautiful orchards and grounds. In these idyllic surroundings, 23-year-old Aleck soon recovered his strength and health. By Christmas, he was itching to get out into the world again.

After setting up a laboratory at Tutelo Heights, Aleck's father had gone on a lecture tour around eastern Canada and the U.S. While in Boston, Massachusetts, he found a job for Aleck teaching at the Boston School for Deaf Mutes.

Aleck loved Boston's air of enthusiasm and opportunity. He was a skilled teacher, whose work had a solid scientific

BELOW: *These two maps show where Alexander Graham Bell spent most of his life, first in Scotland and London, and later in Canada and the United States. The inset map shows where these places are in the world.*

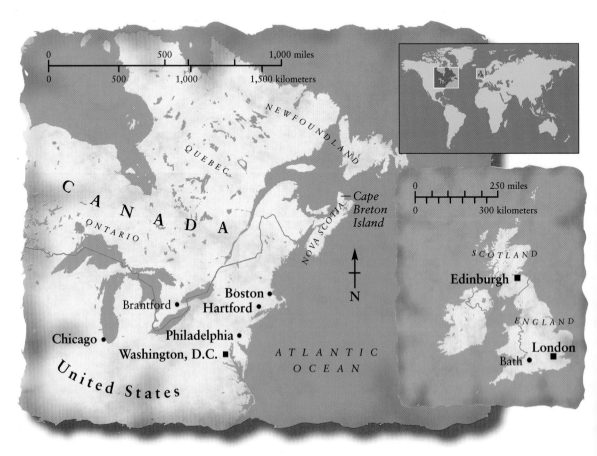

base, and his class of thirty pupils made spectacular progress. Aleck was invited to lecture on his methods and was never short of private pupils to boost his income.

In March 1872, Aleck, now 25 years old, moved to the Clarke School for the Deaf, also in Boston, where he proved a respected and successful teacher once again. The move brought another, more significant reward. A month after he started, Aleck met the school's president, Gardiner Greene Hubbard. Hubbard was a lawyer who specialized in protecting inventions using patents. He also had a 15-year-old daughter, Mabel, who had been deaf since the age of four after an attack of scarlet fever. Hubbard and Bell forged a partnership, founded on a mutual interest in inventions and deafness that changed the young Scotsman's life forever.

IN THEIR OWN WORDS

"I should not personally object to teaching Visible Speech in some well-known institution if you would get an appointment—even if it was not remunerative [paid]."

ALECK WRITING TO HIS FATHER IN BOSTON, ON OCTOBER 28, 1871, ASKING HIM TO FIND HIM A JOB.

LEFT: *Tremont Street, Boston, in the 1860s. Alexander Graham Bell felt at home in the wealthy and expanding American city.*

IN THEIR OWN WORDS

"He moves his hand, with thumb and forefinger close together, slowly from left to right... spreads out his fingers quickly when he wants them to stop. Then he begins again... and such a roar comes up as makes the floor tremble, the windows rattle, and the hall resound again.... The pupils like it. It is a new sensation to most of them....People stop in the street to listen, and stare at the windows. The noise may be heard a quarter of a mile off."

FROM *SILENT WORLD*, A MAGAZINE FOR THE DEAF, ON JUNE 15, 1872, DESCRIBING HOW ALECK WARMED UP HIS CLASS AT THE START OF THE DAY.

THE MULTIPLE TELEGRAPH

The pace of Aleck's life was quickening rapidly. He taught for a while at the American Asylum, Hartford. Then, in September 1871, he opened his own school for deaf pupils in Boston. At the same time, Aleck continued his lecturing, writing, and work with private pupils. In his spare moments he conducted scientific research. The project that loomed largest in his mind was the "multiple telegraph," which was a way of sending several telegraph messages down a wire at the same time. Long-distance wires were expensive to lay, so whoever could find a way of using each one more efficiently would make a fortune.

In 1873, Boston University appointed Alexander Graham Bell a Professor of Vocal Physiology and Elocution. It was a great honor. Aleck, a largely self-taught scientist with few formal qualifications, was now a respected member of Boston's scientific elite. With the professorship came the right to use the facilities of the Massachusetts Institute of Technology (MIT).

RIGHT: *Telegraph lines across the United States Great Plains, in 1885.*

Working with Clarence Blake, an ear specialist, Aleck learned more about the workings of the human ear. He also came across the "phonautograph" machine, which recorded the vibrations of sound as written marks. Although the multiple telegraph still dominated his thinking, the variety of his work proved immensely useful. He was collecting the reservoir of information about sound and electricity that would later enable him to invent the telephone.

Aleck's enormous workload sometimes made him ill with fatigue. However, he continued with private lessons. For one pupil in particular he always had time—Mabel Hubbard, Gardiner Hubbard's pretty teenage daughter. Before long Aleck was seeing her as rather more than a gifted and willing student. He was falling in love.

BELL'S MULTIPLE TELEGRAPH

Bell's idea for a multiple telegraph was based on the ability of an individual tuning fork to vibrate only in response to a certain sound frequency.

His idea was to have a series of tuning forks at the transmitting end and receiving end of the telegraph. The vibration of an individual fork at the transmitting end would be converted into a series of electric pulses, which passed down a wire and set in motion the corresponding fork (but no other) at the receiving end.

The importance of this idea was that it led Bell toward the telephone.

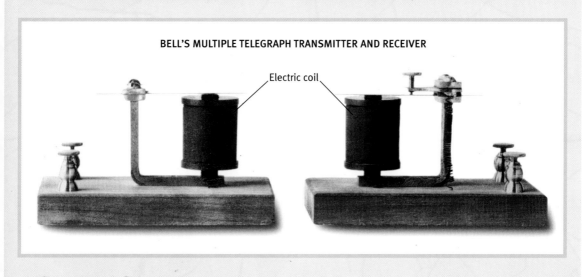

BELL'S MULTIPLE TELEGRAPH TRANSMITTER AND RECEIVER

Electric coil

THE TELEPHONE

The word "telephone" comes from the Greek words meaning "far-sound." For many years, it meant mechanical devices for transmitting speech, such as speaking tubes. However, by the 1870s, it was beginning to be used for machines that transmitted sound by means of electricity.

Aleck thought about the electrical telephone while working on his multiple telegraph. From time to time it caught his imagination, but he set it aside because he was too busy. In July 1874, while enjoying a summer break at Brantford, Ontario, he had time to think carefully about it again.

To send the human voice using electricity, Aleck had to solve three problems: 1) transmit sound as an electrical signal, 2) translate the signal back into sound, and 3) carry out these processes with the complex sound of the human voice. While Aleck was sitting in his "dreaming place," a quiet outcrop overlooking the Grand River, a solution to part of the problem of the telephone suddenly came to him: electrical induction. This meant using a continually flowing current, but varying in power, rather than the pulsating current of the telegraph.

RIGHT: *Thomas Watson (1854–1934), the engineer who worked with Bell on his telephone. Watson's skill with his hands and Bell's inventive genius made an ideal partnership.*

IN THEIR OWN WORDS

"I have scarce dared to breathe [about my idea] to anybody for fear of being thought insane."

ALECK WRITING TO HIS PARENTS ABOUT HIS IDEA OF HARNESSING ELECTRICAL INDUCTION, ON NOVEMBER 23, 1874.

From now on, Aleck became almost obsessed with his telephone idea. However, he was not alone in his search. Other scientists, notably Elisha Gray, were following similar paths. Gray had already produced a machine that could transmit simple music. The quest for the first working telephone was becoming a race.

By early 1875, Aleck had teamed up with Thomas Watson, a young electrician and model maker. Watson proved expert at making whatever apparatus Aleck needed. Equally important, Aleck went into partnership with Gardiner Hubbard and Thomas Sanders. Aleck provided ideas, while his partners gave financial backing and legal advice.

ABOVE: *A pair of Bell telephones, one for speaking into and one for listening from, made in 1877.*

BELOW: *A reproduction of the device Bell first used to translate the sound of the human voice into a variable electric current.*

ABOVE: *Joseph Henry (1797–1878), the American physicist who encouraged Bell and advised him to keep his work on the telephone a secret until it could be protected by patent.*

IN THEIR OWN WORDS

"Aleck is a good fellow and, I have no doubt, will make an excellent husband. He is hot-headed but warm-hearted—sentimental, dreamy, and self-absorbed, but sincere and unselfish. He is ambitious, to a fault, and is apt to let enthusiasm run away with judgement."

IN A LETTER FROM ALECK'S FATHER, ALEXANDER MELVILLE BELL, TO MABEL HUBBARD, ON DECEMBER 6, 1875, CONGRATULATING MABEL ON HER ENGAGEMENT TO HIS SON.

BREAKTHROUGH!

By the spring of 1875, Bell and Watson were progressing well. Hubbard, however, was not always impressed. He was more interested in the multiple telegraph and urged Bell to spend more time on it. The young Bell did what he could to keep Hubbard happy, but he was under enormous strain. After spending his days teaching, writing, and lecturing, Bell worked into the night in his laboratory. At times he came close to a breakdown. Sheer determination and the support of others kept him going.

On March 1, his spirits were lifted by an interview with Joseph Henry, of Washington's Smithsonian Institution. Henry was the most respected American scientist of his day. He showed great interest in Aleck's ideas and gave him excellent advice: keep his work a secret until it could be protected by a patent. Mabel's support came soon afterward. On November 25, 1875, Alexander Graham Bell and Mabel Hubbard were engaged to be married.

Everything was starting to go well. The previous June, Bell and Watson had sent complex sounds along a wire using the principle of variable resistance for the transmitter. On March 10, 1876, they became the first people to hear intelligible human speech over the telephone (see pages 4–7 for a description of this event). The two scientists then made their invention

BELL'S TELEPHONE

The human voice produces vibrations in the air which, in turn, produce similar vibrations on a thin sheet, or diaphragm, of iron. In Bell's telephone, a diaphragm is placed near a magnet. The magnet has a coil of wire wound around it. In the sending instrument, or transmitter, the diaphragm vibrates in response to the voice and an electric signal is produced in the coil of wire. The signal travels to the receiving telephone and varies the magnetism, so that the diaphragm there vibrates in the same way, reproducing the original sound.

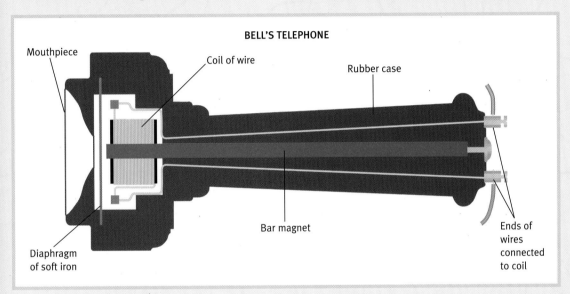

BELL'S TELEPHONE

Mouthpiece

Coil of wire

Rubber case

Diaphragm of soft iron

Bar magnet

Ends of wires connected to coil

more practical by replacing the acid dish and diaphragm with a microphone (just like the receiver). This generated its own current by induction, so there was no need for a separate battery. Three days earlier, the U.S. government had granted a patent for the invention. It would turn out to be one of the most profitable patents ever issued.

IN THEIR OWN WORDS

"I claim, and desire to secure by Letters Patent.... The method of, and apparatus for, transmitting vocal or other sounds telegraphically, as herein described, by causing electrical undulations [waves], similar in form to the vibrations of the air accompanying the said vocal or other sounds."

THE PATENT FOR BELL'S TELEPHONE, U.S. PATENT NO. 174,465, ISSUED ON MARCH 7, 1876.

Marriage and Money

NOW THAT HIS telephone worked, Bell began telling others of his invention. He gave demonstrations to friends, scientific meetings, and the general public. All who heard about the telephone were amazed. The most significant display was at the 1876 Centennial Exhibition in Philadelphia, an event celebrating 100 years since the American Declaration of Independence.

Helped by Thomas Watson, Bell also improved his telephone's sound quality and reliability. Messages were sent several miles using existing telegraph lines. On October 6, 1876, Bell and Watson held the first two-way telephone conversation.

IN THEIR OWN WORDS

"I went into his office this afternoon, and saw him talking to his wife by telephone. He seemed as delighted as could be. The articulation was simply perfect, and they had no difficulty in understanding one another. The first telephone line has now been erected and the telephone is in practical use!"

A LETTER FROM ALECK TO MABEL ON APRIL 4, 1877, DESCRIBING CHARLES WILLIAMS' EXPERIENCE USING THE TELEPHONE IN HIS BOSTON SHOP, ON THE WORLD'S FIRST PERMANENT TELEPHONE LINK.

LEFT: *Bell demonstrating his new invention in Boston, 1877. He is making a telephone call to someone about 144 miles (230 km) away.*

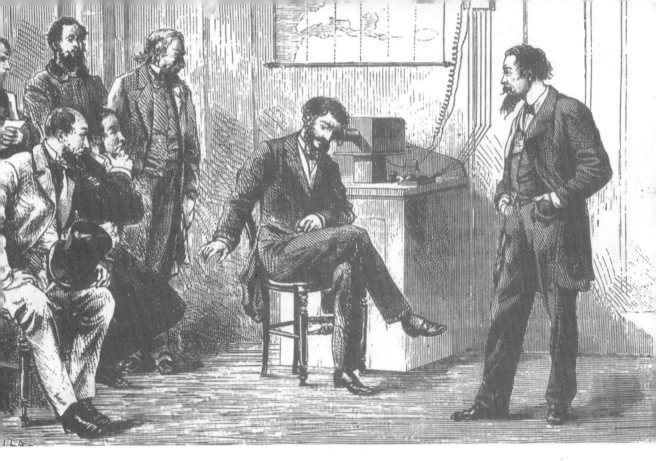

ABOVE: *Quiet please! Thomas Watson, in Boston, receives a telephone call from Alexander Graham Bell in Salem, some 12 1/2 miles (20 km) away. This picture was drawn in 1877.*

Soon people wanted telephone systems installed in their homes and offices, so the instrument started to be manufactured. Meanwhile, the scientist and his assistant continued to demonstrate "talking with electricity" to wider and wider audiences.

After a successful tour around the north-eastern United States in early 1877, Bell was not only famous but he could finally afford to get married. His wedding with Mabel Hubbard took place at her father's house on July 11. After a short honeymoon, the couple left for Europe. Of course, Bell took his telephone apparatus with him.

IN THEIR OWN WORDS

"What a man my husband is! I am perfectly bewildered at the number and size of the ideas with which his head is crammed....Flying machines to which telephones and torpedoes are to be attached occupy the first place just now from observation of seagulls....Then he goes climbing about the rocks and forming theories on the origin of cliffs and caves....Then he comes home and watches sugar bubbles."

A LETTER FROM MABEL HUBBARD TO HER MOTHER,
ON OCTOBER 1, 1877, WHILE TOURING GREAT BRITAIN.

ENGLAND

The Bells stayed on their honeymoon in Europe for a year. Aleck relaxed and put on weight (he burst out of his wedding trousers three times!). He took great pleasure visiting old friends and showing Mabel the haunts of his youth in Scotland. On January 14, 1878, he demonstrated his telephone to Queen Victoria, who warmly appreciated both the invention and its inventor. In London, four months later, Mabel gave birth to a baby daughter, Elsie May Bell. These were happy times.

Legal Battles

Within a year of its invention, it was clear the telephone was going to make a fortune. Realizing this, in July 1877, Bell, Hubbard, Sanders, and Watson had formed the Bell Telephone Company to manufacture and market the new invention.

The company believed, quite correctly, that it was the only company that could make telephones because they had a patent. A great deal of money was involved. Bell had applied for his patent on February 14, 1876. Elisha Gray had applied for a telephone patent on the same day, but two hours later. Gray's backers decided that his patent was just as valid as Bell's.

RIGHT: *Queen Victoria, pictured here, was delighted when Bell demonstrated his telephone to her while on his honeymoon in Britain in 1878.*

ABOVE AND LEFT: *An imaginary telephone conversation between Bell (left) and Elisha Gray (right). This drawing shows their different designs for a telephone.*

Gray was an honest man, but behind him stood a multi-million-dollar enterprise, the Western Union Telegraph Company. Western Union already controlled the telegraph business and was beginning to move into telephones. The Bell Telephone Company claimed that this broke the law because of the Bell patent. In November 1879, a law court upheld the Bell claim. This freed the Bell Telephone Company to make its fortune. Even so, over the next eighteen years, the company had to fight about 600 more legal battles to stop others from stealing its invention.

Aleck was a scientist, not a businessman or a lawyer. He hated the legal arguments and bickering. All he wanted was to receive what was due to him from his telephone and continue with inventing. Dozens of new ideas were already buzzing through his brain. Watching seagulls in Scotland, he had even begun to think of a flying machine.

IN THEIR OWN WORDS

"*The real inventor of the telephone—Mr. Elisha Gray, of Chicago...concerns himself not at all about the spurious [false] claims of Professor Bell....Mr. Gray's claims...are officially approved in the Patent Office at Washington, and they have already brought in large returns in money as well as in reputation to the inventor. Talking by telegraph and other sport of that description Mr. Gray has not paid much attention to as yet.*"

FROM THE *CHICAGO TRIBUNE*, ON FEBRUARY 16, 1877, REFUSING TO ACKNOWLEDGE BELL AS THE FIRST PERSON TO INVENT THE TELEPHONE.

WASHINGTON, D.C.

In October 1878, Aleck and Mabel returned to the United States and began to spend most of their time in Washington, D.C. Money from the telephone company made them very wealthy indeed. This left Aleck free to enjoy his family and get on with other scientific work.

The telephone proved to be only the first of Bell's inventions. In 1880, working with a young assistant, Charles Tainter, he produced what he described as "the greatest invention I have ever made." This was the "photophone," a machine that transmitted sound through light rays. Unfortunately it only worked in good weather conditions, so it wasn't very practical. However, Bell's research laid the foundations for the modern science of lasers and fiber optics.

BELOW: *The transmitter of Bell's "photophone," a device for transmitting speech in the form of a beam of light, which took away the need for wires.*

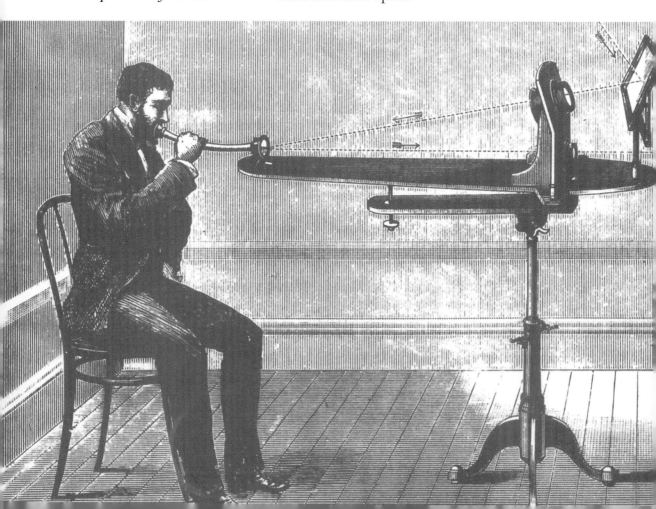

THE GRAPHOPHONE

The graphophone was an instrument that recorded and played back sound. To record sound, a diaphragm at the end of a mouthpiece vibrated when activated by sound. The stylus attached to the diaphragm moved with the vibrations. The stylus scratched the pattern of the vibrations on to a revolving drum covered in wax.

To play back sound, a lighter stylus traced the original marks made on the wax. The stylus operated a receiver diaphragm, which played back the original sound (scratchily).

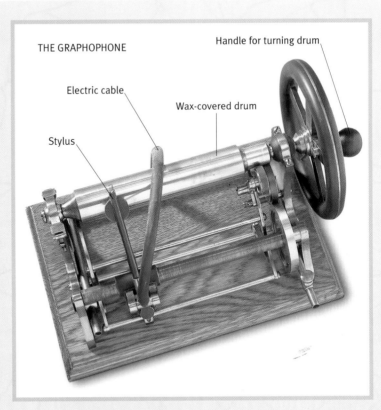

THE GRAPHOPHONE

Electric cable

Stylus

Wax-covered drum

Handle for turning drum

The next year, in 1881, Bell was awarded the $10,000 Volta Prize for his work with electricity. He used the money to set up the Volta Laboratory for experiment and invention. Here, working with Charles Tainter and his cousin Chichester Bell, Aleck invented the "graphophone." The machine, an improvement on Thomas Edison's phonograph (invented in 1878), used a stylus and a wax cylinder to record sound. Its patent (1887) earned the inventors a handsome income for many years.

BELOW: *The photophone receiver.*

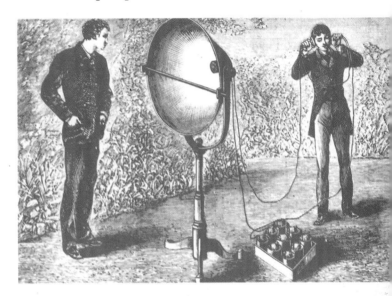

Triumphs and Tragedies

NOT ALL OF Aleck's inventions were so successful. In the summer of 1881, he had received an urgent telephone call summoning him to the White House. His friend President James Garfield had been shot. Aleck tried to find the bullet using a type of electric metal detector that he had invented. For some reason the device did not work and Garfield died in great pain.

Bell never forgot that the road to the telephone had begun with teaching the deaf. In 1883, he set up a day school for deaf children in Washington, D.C. Three years later he established the Volta Bureau as a center for the scientific study of deafness. In 1890, he helped found the American Association to Promote the Teaching of Speech to the Deaf.

Aleck also used his wealth to promote science. In 1883, he and his father-in-law founded the magazine *Science*, to publish details of the latest scientific research. More honors were showered upon him. The same year, after being granted American citizenship at the age of 36, Bell was elected to the U.S. National Academy of Sciences. The distinction was normally granted to scientists after a lifetime of work. In 1897, he became President of the National Geographic Society and pioneered photographs in the society's *National Geographic* magazine.

LEFT: *The shooting of President James Garfield, in 1881, illustrated in a French magazine called* **Le Journal Illustré.**

BESSEMER PUBLIC LIBRARY

Fame meant little to Bell. He was most relaxed when he was with his family, working in his laboratory, or wandering in open countryside outside Washington, D.C. In 1880, the Bells had a second daughter, Marian, also known as Daisy. Their wish for a boy was granted on August 15, 1881, when baby Edward was born. Sadly, he was unable to breathe properly and lived only a few hours. Mabel, a deeply religious woman, believed that Edward's death was a form of punishment from God. Bell did not share his wife's beliefs. In an attempt to come to terms with his misery, he designed a metal "vacuum jacket" to help with breathing. After the early death of a second son, Robert, in 1883, the Bells had no more children.

LEFT: *Alexander Graham Bell and his wife Mabel, who was deaf from the age of four. She was one of the first children in the United States to learn to hold a conversation by lipreading.*

BESSEMER PUBLIC LIBRARY

IN THEIR OWN WORDS

"...books are everywhere. An easy chair lies in front of the fire, and a globe stands in one corner. At a common flat walnut desk, sitting on an office chair cushioned with green leather, Mr. Bell works. The desk is covered with books and papers....A porcelain hand with letters pasted upon it lies at one side, and this, I am told, is an invention for teaching deaf children to converse with each other by touching certain spots on the hand, which represent letters."

FROM THE *AURORA HERALD*, MARCH 12, 1889, DESCRIBING THE INSIDE OF BELL'S STUDY IN HIS WASHINGTON HOUSE.

A SUMMER HOME

In the summer of 1891, the Bells moved into a new, three-story house on Connecticut Avenue, Washington, D.C. It remained their American residence for the rest of their lives. But, for all its comfort, it was not really home.

Six years earlier, in 1885, Bell and his father had visited Cape Breton Island in northern Nova Scotia, Canada. Aleck fell in love with the "gentle restful beauty" of the place. Its lakes and valleys, islands, and cool breezes reminded him very much of his native Scotland. Here, near the town of Baddeck, he decided to establish the Bell family home.

Gradually, over a period of seven years, Bell bought up all the land in the area where he wanted to build his house. In the meantime, he and Mabel rented a summer cottage nearby. Then they spent the warmer months in a newly built lodge. Finally, in 1893, the house they called "Beinn Bhreagh," which is Gaelic for "beautiful mountain," was finished.

IN THEIR OWN WORDS

"Baddeck is certainly possessed of a gentle, restful beauty, and I think we would be content to stay here many weeks..."

MABEL BELL'S ENTRY IN HER JOURNAL ON
SEPTEMBER 17, 1885.

BELOW: *Beinn Bhreagh, the Bells' idyllic home near Baddeck, Nova Scotia, Canada, which they built in the early 1890s.*

ABOVE: *Alexander and Mabel Bell with their daughters Elsie and Marian, in about 1885.*

Beinn Bhreagh was a huge, rambling mansion with accommodations for 26 people and a small army of servants. It had a great hall, with a blazing log fire, a book-lined study, and well-equipped laboratories. On the surrounding estate were cottages, cabins, and boathouses.

For almost the next thirty years, virtually every member of the Bell clan gathered in this glorious summer home— Aleck and Mabel, their parents and daughters, cousins, nephews, nieces, and grandchildren. The cost of running Beinn Bhreagh was enormous but, as Mabel pointed out, the money was unimportant as long as the family was happy.

FLIGHTS OF FANCY

BELOW: *Alexander Graham Bell with one of his tetrahedral (four-sided) kites, in 1904. His experiments with its design proved important for the future development of aeronautics.*

Aleck had never liked the bright lights and social whirl of the city. As he grew older, he became more reclusive. Yet he never lost his youthful energy, compassion, and enthusiasm for new ideas. Since his honeymoon visit to Scotland, Aleck had been interested in flight. For a time he devoted his energies to kites. In the winter of 1901, he invented a four-sided (tetrahedral) kite with triangular panels that combined remarkable strength and lightness. Then, after the Wright brothers' first successful powered flight in 1903, Aleck turned his attention to flying machines capable of carrying people. In 1907, he joined with a group of young enthusiasts—Casey Baldwin, Glenn Curtiss, J.A.D. McCurdy, and Thomas Selfridge—to form the Aerial Experiment Association (AEA). Mabel, who had shared Aleck's wealth from the start, was the business brain behind the Association and put up $20,000 to get it going.

This made the AEA the world's first organization for scientific research that was established and funded by a woman.

By 1909, AEA had produced four airplanes. On February 23, one of them, the Silver Dart, made the first powered flight of a heavier-than-air machine in Canada. Aleck, as always, did not stick to one project at a time. While working on flight, he explored a wide variety of other subjects. These included sheep breeding, using sound waves to examine underwater objects ("sonar detection"), and how the sun's power might be used to get fresh water from the sea.

IN THEIR OWN WORDS

"He is a magnificent figure of a man.... The other evening he danced for us, and whether it was a Scotch jib or a Highland fling, or an original made-up-on-the-spot caper I do not know, but it was a great show."

MABEL BELL'S COUSIN, MARY BLATCHFORD, DESCRIBING ALECK DURING A VISIT TO BEINN BHREAGH IN THE AUTUMN OF 1911.

BELOW: *A devoted couple, the Bells enjoy a peaceful moment together in the garden of their home at Beinn Bhreagh, in 1909.*

FINAL YEARS

Aleck and Mabel were deeply upset when World War I began in the summer of 1914. The couple had traveled widely around the world, learning to appreciate different peoples and cultures. The slaughter of the war saddened them. But Aleck was no pacifist. He was angry that the United States did not join Great Britain and its allies until 1917, and wasn't bothered by the fact that his inventions—most notably the telephone— were used in the conflict.

By the turn of the 20th century, Alexander Graham Bell was the "grand old man" of world science. He had been awarded a dozen honorary doctorates (although he never called himself Dr. Bell) and was presented with scores of medals and other awards. He sometimes grumbled that all this glory was of no use to him now—why hadn't it been given to him when he was a struggling young research scientist?

ABOVE: *An invention for peace and war—a British officer tests a German telephone captured in 1918, during World War I.*

BELOW: *Bell wears headphones as he tests out a new piece of electrical equipment in 1915.*

ABOVE: *A photograph of the Bell-Baldwin HD-4 hydrofoil in action in 1918. This photograph is inside the Bell Museum, in Baddeck, Nova Scotia.*

Bell continued inventing. During the war, based at Beinn Bhreagh, he and Casey Baldwin developed their own version of the hydrofoil, first successfully invented in 1906. This new type of high-speed boat was fitted with underwater "wings" that lifted the hull clear of the water as it gathered speed. In September 1919, the Bell-Baldwin HD-4 hydrofoil, driven by aircraft propellers, reached a world record of 71 1/4 miles (114 km) per hour. The record stood for over ten years.

Aleck was now over seventy and his energy was finally slackening. Weakened by diabetes, by the end of July 1922 he was too feeble to stand. He still continued to dictate his journal, however. On the last day of July, he was urged not to hurry with his dictation. "I have to!" he replied. He was right. Two days later, holding tight to Mabel's hand, he slipped quietly away.

IN THEIR OWN WORDS

"What a glorious thing it is to be young and have a future before you... [But] it is also a glorious thing to be old and look back upon the progress of the world during one's own lifetime.... I, myself, am not so very old yet, but I can remember the days when there were no telephones."

ALEXANDER GRAHAM BELL, TALKING TO A GATHERING OF GRADUATES IN 1917, QUOTED IN THE *NATIONAL GEOGRAPHIC* MAGAZINE, FEBRUARY 1917.

The Legacy of Bell

ALEXANDER GRAHAM BELL left a rare legacy, as both a human being and a scientist. Despite his wealth and his fame, he never forgot those less fortunate than himself. He funded deaf schools, gave money for research into deafness, kept in touch with ex-pupils, and even taught the occasional class.

A devoted family man, Bell spent much of his money on providing a secure home for all the clan. His father, Alexander Melville Bell, spent his final years at Beinn Bhreagh and died there in 1905. He supported his daughter Elsie's husband, Gilbert Grosvenor, as a writer and Daisy's husband, David Fairchild, as a botanist. Many other young people, especially the inventor Casey Baldwin, benefited from Bell's friendship and help.

Bell's scientific legacy was equally remarkable. His patents covered fields as varied as telephones and telegraphs, the photophone, aircraft, hydrofoils, and improved batteries. More interested in ideas than practical matters, he left many projects unfinished. His research into light is still being developed in laser and fiber-optic technology.

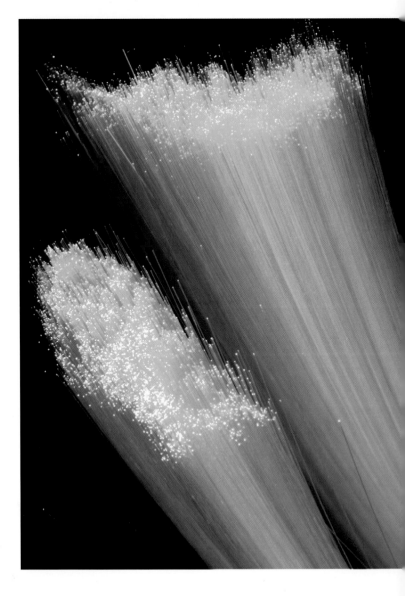

BELOW: *Fiber-optic cables, a modern development from the experimental work done by one of the most gifted inventors of recent times—Alexander Graham Bell.*

Bell believed scientific knowledge coupled with a concern for others would bring undreamed of benefits to all humanity. His greatest legacy, the telephone, reflected this belief. It changed the way we live, bringing swift help to the sick and injured, comfort to the lonely, and drawing people everywhere closer together.

ABOVE: *A modern hydrofoil in use as a ferry among the Greek islands, 1985.*

BELOW: *Telephones have come a long way from Bell's first device that sent speech electrically down a wire.*

IN THEIR OWN WORDS

"Gifted with a voice that itself suggested genius, he spoke the English language with a purity and charm which have never been surpassed by anyone I have heard speak....Dr. Bell had a happy way of making people feel pleased with themselves. He had a remarkable faculty of bringing out the best that was in them."

ANNIE SULLIVAN, WHO FIRST MET ALECK IN 1887, SPEAKING ABOUT HIM AFTER HIS DEATH. FROM *ANNE SULLIVAN MACY* BY NELLA BRADDY (GARDEN CITY, NEW YORK, 1933).

Timeline

1837
Sir Charles Wheatstone and Sir William Cooke (Great Britain) and Samuel Morse (U.S.) invent the telegraph.

1847
MARCH 3: Alexander Bell is born in Edinburgh, Scotland.

1858
Aleck takes the name "Graham" to become Alexander Graham Bell.

1858-62
Aleck attends the Royal High School, Edinburgh.

1862-63
Aleck visits his grandfather in London.

1863
Aleck begins teaching at Weston House Academy, Elgin, Scotland.

1864
Alexander Melville Bell develops Visible Speech. Aleck attends classes at Edinburgh University for a few weeks.

1865-66
Aleck teaches at Elgin again and conducts his first experiments with sound.

1866-67
Aleck teaches at Somersetshire College, Bath, England.

1867
Edward Bell dies of tuberculosis. Alexander Melville Bell publishes *The Science of Universal Alphabetics* explaining his Visible Speech program.

1868
Aleck teaches speech to the deaf at Susanna Hull's school, London, and attends classes at University College, London.

1870
Melville Bell dies of tuberculosis. The Bell family emigrates to Canada.

1871
Aleck teaches at the Boston School for Deaf Mutes.

1872
Aleck meets Gardiner Greene Hubbard, his future backer and father-in-law. Opens his own school for the deaf in Boston and experiments with the multiple telegraph.

1873
Bell is appointed Professor of Vocal Physiology and Elocution at Boston University. Accepts Mabel Hubbard as a private pupil.

1874
Bell experiments with sound at the Massachusetts Institute of Technology and first thinks of the idea for a telephone. Begins working with Thomas Watson.

1875
Bell sets up a partnership with Thomas Sanders and Gardiner Hubbard, receives encouragement from Joseph Henry of the Smithsonian Institution, and becomes engaged to Mabel Hubbard.

1876
FEBRUARY: Bell applies for a patent for the telephone, two hours before Elisha Gray. MARCH 7: Telephone patent is granted by the U.S. government. MARCH 10: Bell and Watson hear intelligible human speech over the telephone for the first time. JUNE: Bell demonstrates his telephone at the Centennial Exhibition, Philadelphia.

1877
The Bell Telephone Company is formed. Bell marries Mabel Hubbard. Thomas Edison invents the phonograph.

1877-78
Aleck and Mabel tour Europe.

1878
Elsie May Bell is born.

1879
Law court upholds Bell's telephone patent.

1880

Marian ("Daisy") Bell is born.
Bell invents the photophone with
Charles Sumner Tainter.
Bell is awarded the Volta Prize by
the French government. Sets up
the Volta Laboratory.

1881

Alexander Bell, Chichester Bell,
and Charles Tainter improve
the phonograph.
Bell fails to save
President Garfield.
Edward Bell dies in infancy.

1882

Bell is granted
American citizenship.

1883

Bell sets up a school for deaf
children in Washington, D.C., is
elected to the National Academy
of Sciences, and sets up the journal *Science* with Hubbard.
Robert Bell dies in infancy.

1886

Bell sets up the Volta Bureau for
studies into deafness. Begins
buying land on Cape Breton
Island, Nova Scotia.

1887

The graphophone is patented.

1890

Bell helps form the American
Association to Promote the
Teaching of Speech to the Deaf.

1892

Bell opens a telephone line
between New York and Chicago.

1893

Beinn Bhreagh is finished on
Cape Breton Island, Nova Scotia.
Bell is elected President of the
National Geographic Society upon
the death of Gardiner Hubbard.
Guglielmo Marconi transmits
radio signals several miles.

1898

Bell becomes regent of the
Smithsonian Institution.

1900

Elsie Bell marries Gilbert
Grosvenor, editor of the
National Geographic magazine.

1901

Bell invents the tetrahedral kite.

1903

Wright brothers make the
first powered flight by a
heavier-than-air machine.

1905

Marion ("Daisy") Bell marries
David Fairchild.

1907

Mabel Bell funds the Aerial
Experiment Association (AEA). The
members were her husband, Casey
Baldwin, Glenn Curtiss, J.A.D.
McCurdy, and Thomas Selfridge.

1909

AEA's Silver Dart makes the first
powered flight in Canada.

1914–18

World War I

1915

Bell opens the trans–America
telephone line by talking from
New York to Thomas Watson
in San Francisco.

1917

The United States enters
World War I.

1919

Bell's HD-4 hydrofoil craft sets
the world marine speed record.

1922

AUGUST 2: Alexander Graham
Bell dies at Beinn Bhreagh.

1923

Mabel Bell dies.

Glossary

Acid Chemical that eats into many other substances. Vinegar, for example, is a weak acid; sulphuric acid is a strong one.

Circuit (SUR-kit) Path of an electric current.

Diaphragm (DYE-uh-fram) Thin sheet of material stretched over an opening.

Doctorate (DOC-tur-et) Highest form of university degree. Those with a doctorate are called "doctor."

Electromagnet (i-LEK-troh-MAG-nit) Magnet made by a coil of wire through which electricity passes.

Elocution (el-uh-KYOO-shuhn) Art of speaking clearly.

Emigrate (EM-uh-grate) To go and live in another country, usually overseas.

Fiber optics (FYE-bur OP-tiks) Science of passing light down a glass or plastic wire.

Graphophone (GRA-fuh-fone) Machine for recording and playing back sound on a drum or disk.

Hydrofoil (HYE-druh-foil) Boat fitted with underwater "wings" that lift the hull clear of the water.

Industrial Revolution (in-DUHSS-tree-uhl rev-uh-LOO-shuhn) Period in the 18th and 19th centuries when, in many Western countries, manufacturing became more important than agriculture.

Morse Code System of sending messages by short (dots) and long (dashes) signals.

Multiple telegraph (MUHL-tuh-puhl TEL-uh-graf) System of sending several telegraph messages down the same wire.

Mute Unable to speak.

Pacifist (PASS-uh-fist) Someone opposed to war who refuses to fight.

Patent (PAT-uhnt) Official document that registers an idea as someone's property. Other people may not use it without permission from the owner of the patent.

Phonautograph (fone-AW-toh-graf) Machine for recording sound as visible marks.

Phonograph Earliest form of gramophone.

Photophone Bell's machine for transmitting sound through light rays.

Physics (FIZ-iks) Study of matter and energy, particularly heat, light, and sound.

Physiology (FI-zee-o-luh-jee) Study of the makeup of the human body.

Pitch The position of a musical note on the scale.

Stylus (STI-luhs) Gramophone needle.

Telegraph Machine for sending electrical messages down a wire.

Transmit To send an electrical message.

Tuning fork (toon-ing fork) Metal fork that always makes the same note when struck.

Variable resistance (VAIR-ee-uh-buhl ri-ZISS-tuhnss) Means of varying the strength of an electrical current. In Bell's first telephone, this was done by varying the distance a current passed through dilute acid.

Visible Speech (VIZ-uh-buhl speech) Alexander Melville Bell's system for teaching the deaf to speak.

Further Information

BOOKS FOR YOUNGER READERS

Fisher, Everett Leonard. *Alexander Graham Bell.* New York: Atheneum, 1999.

Gearhart, Sarah. *The Telephone: Turning Point Inventions.* New York: Atheneum, 1999.

MacLeod, Elizabeth. *Alexander Graham Bell: An Inventive Life.* Canada: Kids Can Press, 1999.

Parker, Steve. *Alexander Graham Bell and the Telephone.* Broomall, PA: Chelsea House, 1994.

Pasachoff, Naomi. *Alexander Graham Bell: Making Connections.* New York: Oxford University Press, 1998.

Schuman, Michael A. *Alexander Graham Bell: Inventor and Teacher.* Connecticut: Blackbirch Press, 2000.

Shuter, Jane. *Lives and Times: Alexander Graham Bell.* Connecticut: Heinemann, 2000.

BOOKS FOR OLDER READERS:

Bruce, Robert V. *Alexander Graham Bell and the Conquest of Solitude.* New York: Cornell University Press, 1990.

Grosvenor, Edwin S., Morgan Weeson, Robert V. Bruce. *Alexander Graham Bell.* New York: Harry N. Abrams Inc., 1997.

WEBSITES

There are hundreds of websites about Bell. A few are really useful, but most have nothing to do with the famous scientist. Trusted organizations like the BBC, the Library of Congress, and universities have sites you can rely on. If you are unsure about a site, ask an adult.

Here are a few useful sites to start from:

http://campus.northpark.edu/history//WebChron/Technology/AGBell.html

http://memory.loc.gov/ammem/bellhtml/bellhome.html

http://www.att.com/technology/forstudents/brainspin/alexbell/

http://www.fitzgeraldstudio.com/html/bell/theman.html

http://www.invent.org/book/book-text/7.html

http://www.pbs.org/wgbh/amex/telephone/peopleevents/mabell.html

Index

Page numbers in **bold** are pages where there is a photograph or an illustration.

© 2001 White-Thomson Publishing Ltd.

BESSEMER PUBLIC LIBRARY